Poems From Co Durham
Edited by Mark Richardson

 Young**Writers**

First published in Great Britain in 2007 by:
Young Writers
Remus House
Coltsfoot Drive
Peterborough
PE2 9JX
Telephone: 01733 890066
Website: www.youngwriters.co.uk

SB ISBN 978-1 84431 258 0

Foreword

Young Writers was established in 1991 and has been passionately devoted to the promotion of reading and writing in children and young adults ever since. The quest continues today. Young Writers remains as committed to the nurturing of poetic and literary talent as ever.

This year's Young Writers competition has proven as vibrant and dynamic as ever and we are delighted to present a showcase of the best poetry from across the UK and in some cases overseas. Each poem has been selected from a wealth of *Little Laureates* entries before ultimately being published in this, our sixteenth primary school poetry series.

Once again, we have been supremely impressed by the overall quality of the entries we have received. The imagination, energy and creativity which has gone into each young writer's entry made choosing the poems a challenging and often difficult but ultimately hugely rewarding task - the general high standard of the work submitted ensured this opportunity to bring their poetry to a larger appreciative audience.

We sincerely hope you are pleased with this final collection and that you will enjoy *Little Laureates Poems From Co Durham* for many years to come.

Contents

Holleigh Lowery (11)   37
Jamie Carty (11)   38
Rebecca Rochester (11)   39
Paul Bloomfield (10)   40
Paul Rickaby (10)   41
Alice Morton (10)   42
Melissa Henderson (11)   43
Erin Scott (11)   44
Christian Marshall (11)   45
Danielle Hall (11)   46
Luke Foster (11)   47
Natasha Stones (11)   48
Courtney Price (10)   49

Middlestone Moor Junior School
Molly Lickley (10)   50
Adam Sutherland (10)   51
Adam Moore (10)   52
Michaela Wright (10)   53
Sapphire Demirsöz (9)   54
Sophie Hawkins & Amy Hawkins (10)   55
Katelyn English (10)   56
Saffi Hutchinson (10)   57
PJ Chatterton (9)   58
Emily Richards (10)   59
Rhys Halpin (9)   60
Matthew Geldart (9)   61
Conor Kirkby (10)   62
Cadam Quinn (10)   63

St Augustine's RC Primary School, Darlington
Christina Turnbull (10)   64
Courtney Nicholson (10)   65
Christian Potter (10)   66
Patrick Dunstall (10)   67
Christian Brown (9)   68
Adam Walters (9)   69
Reuben Oatley (9)   70
Victoria Lindsay (11)   71
Elena Dunstall (11)   72
James Gillow (10)   73

Katie Noble (11)	74
Heather Randle (10)	75
Callum Adair (10)	76
Emily Noble (10)	77
Chloe Outterson (10)	78
Rosie Pilling (9)	79
Katie Newton (11)	80
Sophie Bainbridge (10)	81

St Bede's RC Primary School, Darlington

Laura Hustwick (11)	82
Conner Hamilton (11)	83
Anna Reed (11)	84
Loren Bell (11)	85
Adam Tombling (11)	86
Leon Cunningham (10)	87
Eleanor Thirlway (11)	88
Robert Spereall (11)	89
Lucy Robson (10)	90
Summer Hanson (10)	92
Rose Passman (11)	93
Emma Reid (11)	94
Kate Blakeborough (11)	95

St Joseph's RC (VA) Primary School, Stanley

Andrew Kitchen (11)	96
Sarah Young (11)	97
Katy Robson (11)	98
Hannah True (11)	99
Jack McCrea (11)	100
Emily Wilson-James (11)	101
Adam Caulfield (10)	102
Bethany Wilkins (11)	103
Adam Thompson (11)	104
Rachael Cowan (11)	105
Daniel Connor (11)	106
Luke Tulip (11)	107
Andrew Connor (11)	108
Jonathan Grey (11)	109

St William's RC (VA) Primary School, Trimdon Station

Shalu James (10)	110
Elise Brown (9)	111
Alix Payne (9)	112
Emeka Ononeze (10)	113
Basma Cherradi (9)	114
Rebecca Dentith (10)	115
Jessica Storey (11)	116
Brad Langley Thompson (10)	117
Martin Worthington (11)	118
Matthew Bennett (11)	119
Ciaran Jasper (11)	120
Mark Ellis (11)	121
Harry Sheldon (10)	122
John Ashurst (11)	123
Mark Allaway (9)	124
Liam Cairns-Smith (9)	125
Joseph Worley (10)	126
Courtney Turnbull (9)	127
Jordan Gavin (11)	128
Sarah Cant (11)	129
Rebecca Spellman (10)	130

The Poems

Best Friends

B is for best friends for life and beyond
E is for ever and ever we will be best friends
S is for spooky sleepovers we have
T is for Terri Pyle (my best friend)

F is for the brilliant friendship we have
R is for the relationship we have together
I is for interesting times we have together
E is for exciting times we have all the time
N is for the never-ending time we have been best friends
D is for dares we play all the time when we are together
S is for sad times we have had together.

Katie McKee (11)
Dene House Primary School

Best Friends

B is for my best friends
E is for every secret we share
S is for smiles we give each other
T is for the truth we share

F is for my best friends, Katie and Lucy
R is for a relationship we share
I is for interesting times we have together
E is for the enjoyable times we have had
N is for you'll never split us up
D is for disasters we've lived through
S is for sad times we've been through.

Terri Pyle (11)
Dene House Primary School

My Dreamland

In my dreams, I swoop away on a magic carpet.
I see
Dragons and dinosaurs,
Fish and forests,
I travel through
The deepest, darkest ocean,
Over the highest mountain,
Through prehistoric lands,
Never forgotten.

In my dreams, I fly through the stars,
Through polar lands and glistening caves
In lonely, empty outer space,
All alone in my heavy daze.
My monkey Jojo and I explore the world together,
Never alone and always together - forever,
In my dreams.

Lucy Parkin (11)
Dene House Primary School

The Leopard

I don't know what you think about,
Leopards long, short or stout,
But I think they are very nice,
Better than your boring pet mice,
For I did, once, see a leopard,
Stalking sheep left by the shepherd.
It crawled low - almost lying,
Then it jumped, the sheep was crying
For its shepherd - over there,
But he wouldn't listen, he didn't care.
The leopard slowly attacked the sheep,
Making the poor creature weep
For its father or its mother,
It wanted support from one or the other.
But neither of them heard his cry
And soon enough, the sheep had died.
The leopard yawned, baring his teeth,
Gritted with blood from the meat!
Then carefully he leaped up a tree
To have his afternoon sleep,
Now do you see why I find
This creature to stay in my mind?
I hope you do - for I love it,
Though if you don't care one little bit,
You must be soft and very sappy,
Though if this part keeps you happy,
The next poem that I shall write
Will be about your boring pet mice!

Rebecca Walters (11)
Dene House Primary School

My Grandad

S is for sad times with my grandad
A is for the always loving grandad
D is for the death of my grandad

T is for the good times with my grandad
I is for the insane times with my grandad
M is for me and my grandad
E is for the excellent advice from Grandad
S is for the special times with my grandad.

Christopher Newhouse (11)
Dene House Primary School

Sadness

S is for seeing my great uncle lying dead
A is for agreeing not to talk about his sudden death
D is for the horrible sudden death of my great uncle
N is for the nice times that we had together
E is for the exciting times I enjoyed with him
S is for the sadness of my great uncle's death
S is for sorry that my great uncle died.

Louis Robbins (11)
Dene House Primary School

My Magic Box

(Inspired by 'Magic Box' by Kit Wright)

In my box you will hear . . .
The sound of angels singing away,
The calling of seagulls as they fly to the bay,
The first breath of life as a baby is born.

In my box you will smell . . .
The scent of a blossom tree,
The smell of a Sunday roast,
The smell of roses on a damp day.

In my box you will see . . .
The flutter of birds as they fly around me,
The first step of a baby
As its mother holds its hand,
The laughter of children playing in the sand.

What will you put in your magic box?

Bethany Smith (10)
Dene House Primary School

Magic Box

(Based on 'Magic Box' by Kit Wright)

In my magic box I will put . . .
The singing of a morning bird,
The sound of children playing,
The gurgle of babies' laughter,
The revving of a car's engine.

In my magic box I will put . . .
The scent of roses on a damp morning,
The smell of an apple - freshly squeezed,
The aroma of chicken roasting in the oven,
The smell of sweet, fresh air.

In my magic box I will put . . .
The tender touch of the softest silk,
The feel of animals' fur,
The touch of a baby's soft smooth skin,
The crunch of grass on a frosty morning.

What will you put in your magic box?

Kevin Pyle (11)
Dene House Primary School

My Magic Box

(Inspired by 'Magic Box' by Kit Wright)

In my magic box you will see . . .
That your dreams are your fantasies,
Your hopes and wishes will come true
As you see the years pass through.

In my magic box you will find . . .
A pink horse and carriage right outside
And a white prom dress sparkling for you.
I'm so excited, what should I do?

In my magic box you will hear . . .
The splashing of the waves as they clash together,
A baby's first footstep to his mother's hands,
The laughter of children, while playing in the sand.

Paige Dinsdale (11)
Dene House Primary School

My Magic Box

(Inspired by 'Magic Box' by Kit Wright)

The touch of a newborn baby,
The giggles of small children,
The smell of freshly-cut grass,
This is what I would like in
My magic box.

The touch of my teddy bear,
The roar of the ocean,
The sweet smell of lilies,
This is what I would like in
My magic box.

The touch of a feather,
The birds chirping in the trees,
The smell of the meadow,
This is what I would like in
My magic box.

Ellen Ruecroft (11)
Dene House Primary School

My Magic Box

(Inspired by 'Magic Box' by Kit Wright)

Inside my box will be . . .
An early morning sunrise,
A daily glowing star,
All four seasons of the year,
A juicy jam jar.

Inside my box will be . . .
My mother's sweet, soft voice,
The sound of my dog's bark,
The first star of a purple-skied night,
The sound of a seeking lark.

Inside my box will be . . .
The smell of a red, red rose,
The sound of popping popcorn,
And now it's time to close . . .
My wonderful magic box!

Charlotte Legg (11)
Dene House Primary School

My Magic Box

(Inspired by 'Magic Box' by Kit Wright)

I will place in my box . . .
The touch of a baby rabbit's fur
The smell of apple crumble, fresh from the oven
The sight of my dog bounding up the path to me
The sound of the blackbird calling the new day
The taste of chocolate melting on my tongue

I will put in my box . . .
The smile on my sister's face when she sees me
The mountain tops and their snowy caps
The golden eagle and its call
The wild waves that splash my feet in the summer heat
The moon and stars that inspire me.

I will store these in
My silver and gold
Ice and fire-coated box
With a key never to unlock
My box will keep my secrets safe
And hold my deep desires
This is what is in my magic box.

Courtney Graham (11)
Dene House Primary School

It's Not My Day

The bus is long,
Steven is bored on the way.
The bus breaks down,
The tyre is on fire.
The children are upside down,
The tyre has popped.
I want to go,
I am glad the tyre is ready,
Let's go! Go! Go!
I think I'm going to faint
Because I have lost my packed lunch.
Then I woke up - I was there.

Daniel Green (10)
Easington Colliery Primary School

Richmond

Our bags are packed,
We're waiting in the hall,
We shouted out our numbers,
We're on our way
And moms and dads are with the cries.

Day 1 was fun,
We had to walk uphill
To the top of the castle,
Had our dinner, back to the home.

Day 2, we looked for clues,
Day 3, we went to Easby Abbey,
The remains of the monks.
The monks were good
But not good enough.
Back to home and bed we went.

Day 4, we went swimming,
A lot of fun, to make friends.
Day 5, we were at the town centre,
We were buying lots,
Then we got asked about our knowledge.
Back home for us.

Ryan Newnes (11)
Easington Colliery Primary School

The Funshack

I went to the Funshack,
It was really great.
I played on the slides
And found a new mate.

We both played football
And he would beat me,
We stopped for some juice,
Then counted to three.

When we had gone,
I had to look back.
I kept on moaning
Then I got a big smack.

I went straight to bed
And then fell asleep,
When I got up,
I heard a loud beep.

Christopher Robson (11)
Easington Colliery Primary School

Metroland

On the roller coaster it was so cool,
Guess who loved it? The whole school.

At Metroland it felt like I could fly,
On the swings they took me so high.

Responsibility is what the children lack,
At Metroland we had chips for a snack.

As the waltzer went round and round,
All you could hear was a screaming sound.

As we set off on the bus,
There was no mess, there was no fuss.

Connor Marr (11)
Easington Colliery Primary School

Fun Factory

Metroland was really fun,
Hop on down and get a bun.
I went on all the rides,
But after that I got sick
Because of all those sweets I had to pick.

Whee, whee, the dodgems are cool,
That's why I'm a fool
To go on all those rides.

Rides here, rides there,
I went on the bouncing bear.
He was funny,
Kept on laughing at my bunny.
That's why I went on all those rides.

Courtney Williams (11)
Easington Colliery Primary School

Disneyland

It was so cool when I went to Disneyland.
One day I made a castle out of sand.
The hotel was really, really brilliant,
My bed was the size of a huge elephant.
The rides are amazing, especially Splash Mountain,
You really get wet, you may as well be under a fountain.
I wish you could come and see I have fun,
All you have got to do is book and then it's done!

Ryan Hall (11)
Easington Colliery Primary School

We're Going To Metroland On A Trip

We're going to Metroland,
It's going to be great.
We're nearly there,
We get there faster than a hare.

On the rides we go,
We're almost done.
Time for the swings,
It's like having wings.

Off we go on the dodgems,
I'm going to bump for a show.
We're really hot,
Oh no, it's time to go.

Laura Wort (10)
Easington Colliery Primary School

Going To The Funshack On A School Trip

Go to the Funshack,
In the ball pools,
Play with children,
Lots more schools.

Go on the slides,
Lots of fun,
It's so cool,
We're almost done.

Play the football,
Jump on a trampoline,
Shout and play,
Eat strawberries and cream.

Time to go now,
I'm very sad,
Come again?
Then I'll be glad.

Lewis Armstrong (11)
Easington Colliery Primary School

Metroland

On our way there
We had a great laugh,
Singing our songs,
Going a bit daft.
Got off the bus,
There was a great fuss.
Got on the rides,
Turning and twisting,
They were very fast,
Side t' side, up 'n' down!

Jak Fenwick (11)
Easington Colliery Primary School

Metroland

Metroland is very great,
You can go there with your mate.
Come to Metroland and go on the shows,
These rides will tingle your toes.
There are roller coasters, swings and loads more,
So come in, just open their door.
You will really have a good time,
So come along, it's no crime.
It's a great place to be,
So please come and see
The exciting place at Metroland.
When we see the bus come, we always run,
We're really excited, it's going to be fun.

Adam Jackson (11)
Easington Colliery Primary School

Strike

B owling was fun
O uch, my foot, it hurts
W hat a game
L ane five was to blame
I dropped the ball on my foot
N o one was allowed to leave the bowling place
G oing home, bye-bye. Oh why do we have to go back home?

Laura Hewitson (11)
Easington Colliery Primary School

The Cinema

Our school is going to the cinema
For being ever so good.
We don't mind the movie,
As long as it isn't a dud.

The movie was great,
There was a character called Ken.
If I had to rate,
It would be a *ten!*

Someone is missing,
None of the children.
One of the teachers is missing,
Mrs Cleet is nowhere to be found.

Running after the bus,
Everyone laughing,
Causing a big fuss,
Poor, out of breath, Mrs Cleet.

Shannon Williams (11)
Easington Colliery Primary School

Metroland

Up, down, round and round,
All I could hear was a screaming sound.
One more lap to go.
Will it go faster? I hope so.

On the waltzer it goes fast,
I love it so much I want it to last.
Round and round it goes,
As the wind lifts my toes.

On the swings I nearly lost my shoe,
I was rising so high I could see the queue.
After a while I got dizzy,
When I got off, my hair was frizzy.

Francesca Smith (11)
Easington Colliery Primary School

To Metroland With The School

Metroland is a really good place
That has lots of rides and lots of space.
We all go with the school
Because the place is very cool.

When the bus comes, we push and shove,
'Cause the back of the bus is the place we love!
When we get there we all run
To the best rides that are fun.

We all went on the swings,
Then for a snack ate onion rings.
Then it was time for dinner,
But after that we went on the spinner.

When it was time to go,
We all shouted, *'No! No! No!'*
So we got an extra hour,
But when we got home we had a shower.

July is the time we're always there,
And then we don't have a second to spare.
We don't go if our square is blue,
So be good and you'll go too!

Amie Richardson (11)
Easington Colliery Primary School

Skiing

Away we go to Italy for a week,
Ready to ski on the peak.
On the coach going through the tunnel,
It looks like we are in a deep, dark funnel.
As we arrive, all tired and sick,
We go to our rooms, we don't get to pick.
Time to unpack,
Oh, I have a load of tack.
Time to sleep
And home we weep.
Wake up for my first day,
Off we go skiing today.
Upon the mountain, snow in our face,
Oh the ski lift doesn't have a lot of space.
Back to the hotel, red and flushed,
I laid on my bed and my teddy got crushed.

Natasha Wilson (11)
Easington Colliery Primary School

The Centre For Life

On the bus I was bored.
When we got there, I was thanking the Lord.
We went in, it took a while,
But still I had a smile.
We went in the 'Around the World',
I was swirled.
After, we went in the Dome,
I thought I was alone.
The day was good.
When I got off the bus, I fell in some mud.

Nathan Armstrong (11)
Easington Colliery Primary School

Safety Carousel

Off we go to Peterlee
To learn some safety tips, you see.
When we got in we saw a big red fire engine,
Then the woman shouted, 'Attention!'
We went to see the coastguard and played a little game,
The whales beat the sharks, they were in shame.
'Follow us,' said the police,
That was the girl, Alish.
We learned much more,
But the info went right to the core.
We all went back to school,
The Safety Carousel was cool.

Sarah Hayes (11)
Easington Colliery Primary School

Richmond . . .

9.30, saying goodbyes,
Getting on the bus, it's all a surprise.
Off we went on our big event,
Got there, it's a blur.
Welcomed by Stuart for our stay,
Packed away for another day.
Went downstairs for our lunch.
After our lunch we went to explore,
Got back in and collapsed on the floor.

Rebecca Patterson (11)
Easington Colliery Primary School

The Richmond Trip

Walking, walking everywhere,
Stuart told us how to get there.
Eating our lunch
With a very big *crunch!*

The swimming pool was really cool,
Everyone splashing about in the big pool.
Beckie sitting on the float
Thinking it was a very small boat.

'It's time for bed,'
Mrs Wood said.
Off we go, real slow,
As we didn't want to go.

Hayley Akers (11)
Easington Colliery Primary School

Richmond

Richmond, we went early in the morning,
On the bus it was so, so boring.,
Saying bye to our mams was such a must,
But when we got there it was fuss, fuss, fuss.
Stuart showed us round our home for the week.
On the way to Grinton, the brakes went screech.

Austen Joseph Bentham (11)
Easington Colliery Primary School

The Centre For Life

About 9.15 we were raring to go
To the Centre for Life to see what's on show.
We unloaded from the bus to get there first,
Some people did some back flips, I expected the worst.
We went to the climates to see what we can do,
We went to the city and powered it too.
Next we went to the dome to see in 3D,
We saw a spider, it was really creepy.
We went on the motion ride, me and Daniel used the force,
When we got off, we showed no remorse.
At two we went back home,
And so this is the end of the poem.

Shaun Willis (11)
Easington Colliery Primary School

Richmond Week

Monday morn, and we're ready to go,
We're all just hoping it won't snow.

In the bus, the engine's on,
Just five minutes till we're gone.

Now we're here, having lunch,
All you hear is munch, munch, munch.

Then we went to Billy Bank Wood,
All we saw was lots of wood.

Just about to go to bed,
Look at my feet, they'll be red.

It's Tuesday, we're raring to go,
Because tonight we have a disco.

Wednesday, going orienteering,
This afternoon, we're going swimming.

Thursday, going down the mine,
Won't go to bed till about half-nine.

Friday and we're coming home,
Hope you like this little poem.

Daniel Armstrong (11)
Easington Colliery Primary School

Sports Is My Game

Liam is my name
And cricket is my game.
I hit a six
So I have a Twix
While they find the ball.

Cain is my name
And footie is my game.
I scored a goal
Then fell in a hole
And hurt my leg again.

Aaron is my name
And cricket is my game,
I stopped the ball,
Lucky I'm tall,
Yes, we won the game.

Liam Rose (11)
Easington Colliery Primary School

Sports

Beckie is my name
And football is my game.
Last night I was on a roll,
I even scored a goal.

Jessica is my friend's name
And netball's her game.
The other night I went and watched,
She got pushed around lots.

Natasha is my friend's name
And basketball's her game.
She plays it every day
And always gets her own way.

Becca is my friend's name
And hockey is her game.
Last night she was on a roll,
She even scored a goal.

Beckie Johnson (11)
Easington Colliery Primary School

Skiing

All of us got on the bus
And no one ever made a fuss.
With the sun shining bright,
Through the window there came light.

Now we're on the ferry
Playing on the games,
People are all merry
And Kevin's throwing flames.

We're back on the bus,
Emily's falling asleep,
Kevin's being a wuss
Because he's scared of the beep.

Holleigh Lowery (11)
Easington Colliery Primary School

School!

Be hip! Be hop!
Don't be a fool,
'Cause if you are,
You'll leave school!

Be hip! Be hop!
Go to the top!
And don't you stop!

Be hip! Be hop!
Go to school
'Cause if you don't
You are a fool.

Jamie Carty (11)
Easington Colliery Primary School

Seaside

I went to the seaside,
It was quite a long ride,
The sea and the sand,
It was all over the land.

The sea was very wet,
But my mam was set,
The sand was dry,
I wanted to cry.

It started to rain,
What a pain!
So I went home
And brushed my hair with a comb.

Rebecca Rochester (11)
Easington Colliery Primary School

Metroland

M etroland is great
E ven though it makes me sick
T he rides are fun
R ides are the best part
O n my birthday I went there
L ittle rides for little ones
A musements everywhere
N ever going away from there
D odgems were the best.

Paul Bloomfield (10)
Easington Colliery Primary School

A Great Time In Metroland

M etroland is really great
E veryone here would give it first rate
T he dodgems were the best
R obert put me to the test
O f course I beat him, that is good
L ee told, he got squished like mud
A very good trip, I thought it was great
N ow the time we got to school it was too late
D o you think it was a good choice?

Paul Rickaby (10)
Easington Colliery Primary School

The Food Festival

I went to the food festival
And had a great time there.
I had a chocolate-covered kebab,
It was made with strawberry pears.

I climbed up four walls,
But I still liked the
Chocolate tasting best,
And I listened to some music as well.

Alice Morton (10)
Easington Colliery Primary School

Metroland

M e and my friends are on a fast ride.
E ating in the bar is lush.
T o start with we went on the boat.
R eally high, we went on the roller coaster.
O ther people threw up on the teachers.
L ittle children were scared of the waltzers
A nd so were some of the older kids.
N ever again will Hayley eat before the roller coaster.
D aniel was terrified of the boat and I mean terrified.

Melissa Henderson (11)
Easington Colliery Primary School

America

America is exciting
with all different kinds of rides.
The roller coasters and Micky Mouse
and the all new Highland Tides.

The Tower of Terror also
and Splash Mountain too.
Come along and enjoy all the different rides
whether you're a girl or boy.

So come along to America
your day will sure be fun,
also see the great attractions
and have a nice ice bun.

With all different characters,
Pluto, Goofy and Minnie Mouse,
Donald Duck and Santa Claus
all live in a big red house.

Erin Scott (11)
Easington Colliery Primary School

Our Day At Richmond

In the bus we went,
The driver was a great gent.

It was really cool,
Then luckily we found the swimming pool.

When we got there,
We didn't have enough time for a pear.

First we went to the castle,
What a great big tassel.

The legend of the drummer boy,
He even has a soldier toy.

Christian Marshall (11)
Easington Colliery Primary School

Off We Go To Richmond!

We're all at school, ready to go,
The coach wasn't here - it was too slow!

Getting on the coach, we're all feeling sick,
The boys behind were getting on my wick.

First day we went to Billy Banks Wood,
On the way back we were covered in mud.

Second day we went to Grinton Moor,
When we got there - it smelt like a sewer.

On the third day there we all went swimming,
I thought it was fun - only in the beginning.

After swimming we went to our rooms,
We looked out the window and saw a great big moon.

Danielle Hall (11)
Easington Colliery Primary School

Richmond

Suitcases packed and ready to go,
Parents crying, 'No, no, no.'

Bus rumbling, we were off,
Handing in sweets we weren't allowed to scoff.

At Richmond, the bus rolled in,
Everybody holding a hearty grin.

Unloading the bags in a great big pile,
We had tons as we were staying a while.

Monday, Tuesday, Wednesday too,
Never running out of things to do.

Five days passed, we were back at school,
Going again would be really cool.

Luke Foster (11)
Easington Colliery Primary School

Centre For Life

On the bus we went,
I said something I never meant.

In the Centre for Life
I had seen a knife.

We went to our lunch,
For someone had given me a punch.

In the arcade
I saw Jake.

We went into the dome,
All I thought about was home.

Natasha Stones (11)
Easington Colliery Primary School

We Went To The Pictures

We went to the pictures, it was so cool,
We saw 'Santa Claus 3', and he is a fool.
I nearly fell asleep
In the comfortable seats,
We had sweets and pop, more and more.
We got on the bus and into the seats
And last of all, we left Mrs Cleet.

Courtney Price (10)
Easington Colliery Primary School

Love

Love is red like the hot sweet rose on a summer's night.
Love sounds like the birds singing at sunset.
Love looks like a solid gold love heart.
Love tastes like a sweet plum.
Love smells like a cute little milky baby.
Love reminds me of a pink bunny.

Molly Lickley (10)
Middlestone Moor Junior School

Anger

Anger feels like a mountain of danger building up inside of you.
Anger tastes like a bitter lemon.
Anger sounds like ignorance.
Anger looks like an impossible task.
Anger smells like a bad odour.

Adam Sutherland (10)
Middlestone Moor Junior School

Happiness

Happiness is as blue as the coolest sea.
Happiness tastes like the sweetest sweet.
Happiness sounds like the best piano player.
Happiness smells like fish and chips at the seaside.
Happiness looks like flowers growing in the sun.
Happiness reminds me of flowers and trees in the sun.

Adam Moore (10)
Middlestone Moor Junior School

Happiness

Happiness looks like a shimmering butterfly in the sunlight,
It tastes like a juicy red apple with chocolate on top.
Happiness is red like a rosy tomato in a salad,
It smells like a scented rose in a flowerpot.
Happiness sounds like the sea washing away the shells on a
summer's day.
Happiness reminds me of snow gliding down out of the winter's sky.

Michaela Wright (10)
Middlestone Moor Junior School

Sadness

The tear drops down from my eye,
My sadness is grey like the many pebbles
Floating away in the ocean.
My heart feels like it's melting away, so I swallow.
I can hear their voices whistling around me,
So I fall to the floor.
I can see their faces and smell their scents,
Which makes me cry even more.
I feel so bad but I can't dry my eyes
With all these tears that I cry.

Sapphire Demirsöz (9)
Middlestone Moor Junior School

Fear

Fear is black like a path of death.
Fear looks like the page of doom going down the Devil's lair.
Fear tastes like rotten eggs with sugar stuffed on top.
Fear smells like you're trapped in the dark, gloomy cage.
Fear sounds like nothing, you're all alone in the world,
                                    nowhere near home.
Fear reminds me of the time when I nearly died.

Sophie Hawkins & Amy Hawkins (10)
Middlestone Moor Junior School

Anger

Anger is red like a charging bull's eyes.
Anger tastes like a burnt meal.
Anger smells like a fire.
Anger sounds like a dark stormy night.
Anger looks like waves hitting the rocks.
Anger reminds me of a storm.

Katelyn English (10)
Middlestone Moor Junior School

Sadness

Sadness is grey like the greyest water storm.
Sadness tastes like a crying tear.
Sadness sounds like a salty, stormy sea.
Sadness reminds you of people passing away.
Sadness smells like a misty raindrop.

Saffi Hutchinson (10)
Middlestone Moor Junior School

Hate

Hate is black like a rain cloud in the sky.
Hate looks like a ball of fire.
Hate sounds like booming drums.
Hate smells like salty water.
Hate tastes like fiery-red spices.

PJ Chatterton (9)
Middlestone Moor Junior School

Sadness

Sadness is blue like a cold, lonely heart.
Sadness tastes like a tear dripping down my face.
Sadness smells like little babies crying.
Sadness looks like a dying flower that has been left for days.
Sadness reminds me of all the lonely people who have no food.

Emily Richards (10)
Middlestone Moor Junior School

Sadness

Sadness is grey like a cloud floating over the greyest fog.
It tastes like the sourest lemon and
Looks like a tear rolling down someone's face.
It smells like a dead rat and
Reminds me of when I fell in the river.

Rhys Halpin (9)
Middlestone Moor Junior School

Fear

Fear is black like a train track.
Fear sounds like cold, dripping blood of human flesh.
Fear smells like sweat before a Premiership game.
Fear looks like a man getting hanged.
Fear tastes like an uncooked mushroom.
Fear reminds me of blazing fire.

Matthew Geldart (9)
Middlestone Moor Junior School

Fear

Fear is like grey weeds lying dead in the garden.
Fear tastes like lava.
Fear smells like a sweaty band.
Fear sounds like a galloping horse coming towards me.
Fear looks like me high up in the sky.
Fear reminds me of bats.

Conor Kirkby (10)
Middlestone Moor Junior School

Love!

Love smells like a milky baby.
Love looks like a married couple.
Love tastes like a leaf shaped like candyfloss.
It sounds like a baby laughing.
It reminds me of a puppy dog.

Cadam Quinn (10)
Middlestone Moor Junior School

Horses

H aving fun all day long
O r riding along the beach with the sun in your hair
R iding, trotting, I like them all
S itting on its back, straight and tall
E ating, that's what they like doing
S lowly halting after a long day of fun!

Christina Turnbull (10)
St Augustine's RC Primary School, Darlington

My Friend Chloe

My friend Chloe, she's really bubbly,
She always talks a lot.
My friend Chloe, she's always hungry,
She moans and moans for food.

My friend Chloe, she's always sleepy,
She wants to go to bed.
My friend Chloe, she's sometimes angry,
You don't want that to happen.

My friend Chloe, she's sometimes funny,
When she pulls some faces.
My friend Chloe, she's my best buddy
And she will be forever!

Courtney Nicholson (10)
St Augustine's RC Primary School, Darlington

My Colourful Parrot

My colourful parrot
Is so bright,
He almost dazzles your sight.
He's red, blue, yellow and green
And his beak is one big fighting machine.
He's turquoise and brown
And aquamarine,
Ivory, black and emerald green.

In his mind and his little black eye,
Who knows what he sees
Beyond the sky
Huge, tall trees, bushes and flowers,
Monkeys and jaguars and rain for hours.
Now to me the gift he gives
Is the colour of the rainforest
Where he might have lived.

Christian Potter (10)
St Augustine's RC Primary School, Darlington

Going On A Bug Hunt

I'm going for a bug hunt
Down in the garden
I wonder what I'll find?

Maybe a woodlouse
Maybe a butterfly
Maybe an ant

I've got a special hoover
To suck up all the bugs
I hope I find a bug today

Hey, cool, I got one!

Patrick Dunstall (10)
St Augustine's RC Primary School, Darlington

When I Went To The Circus

When I went to the circus,
There were blue balloons,
Also funny games
With stupid clowns.

I went on a big wheel,
Also small games.
I saw the lions had been tamed.
I saw the tightrope-walker walking.

When it got to the end
They all packed away.
We were very sad.
We all went home with a smile on our faces.

Christian Brown (9)
St Augustine's RC Primary School, Darlington

The Colour Blue

It reminds me of the sea,
The sky is blue,
Some sweets are blue,
Even some birds are blue.

Even violets are blue.
Are some of your clothes blue?
There are even some blue pens,
So some writing is blue.

Adam Walters (9)
St Augustine's RC Primary School, Darlington

Hamtaro

Hamtaro is very small but very cute
Hamtaro is very nice and very cool
Hamtaro is caring as always
Hamtaro is so kind,
I like him very much

Hamtaro is small and cute, he does very well
Hamtaro is nice and cool, he does very well
Hamtaro is caring as he is.

Reuben Oatley (9)
St Augustine's RC Primary School, Darlington

A Two-Faced Pig

Is she beauty or beast I hear you say,
Look again and your mind will sway.
Could her face be in a pig's tummy,
Or is she brown-haired like a regular mummy?

She holds you in a spell that's her charm,
Should she live in a house or down on a farm?
She sometimes has wings and not pig's feet,
You should see her fly, it's really neat.

Some things aren't always as they seem,
Close your eyes, relax and dream.
My pig's with a double view,
Will always keep her eyes on you.

Victoria Lindsay (11)
St Augustine's RC Primary School, Darlington

What Shall We Have?

The sun is rising
And the birds are singing,
Let's have a picnic
In the countryside.

With jam sandwiches
And champagne,
Or maybe not,
But what shall we have?

I know what we shall have,
Marmalade sandwiches
And wine,
Yes, that'll be fine.

Elena Dunstall (11)
St Augustine's RC Primary School, Darlington

Highway To Hell

The highway to Hell is where all the witches
Start their race.
The ref witch says, 'Ready, steady, go,'
And off they go, racing over the town,
Into Hell!
The screams sound like doors creaking,
Cats fall off brooms, it is so fast.
This is Hell.

James Gillow (10)
St Augustine's RC Primary School, Darlington

No, I'm Busy

'Come on Jane, time to get up.'
'Give me five more minutes Mum.'

'Will you come and tidy up this mess Jane?'
'Can't you Mum? I'm busy.'

'Come and set the table Janey.'
'No Mum, I'll do it tomorrow.'

'Mum, will you give me a lift into town?'
'No, I'm busy.'

Katie Noble (11)
St Augustine's RC Primary School, Darlington

My Holiday

My holiday was the best,
I was in the pool all day
Playing water polo and other water games
With all my friends

Dancing and singing all night long
Doing the karaoke
And the conga
It was a lot of fun

I came back very brown
And all my friends were jealous of me
I brought my class some sweets
And my friends some gifts back.

Heather Randle (10)
St Augustine's RC Primary School, Darlington

Donkeys

Donkeys, donkeys at a funfair,
Donkeys, donkeys on a roller coaster,
Donkeys, donkeys having ice cream,
How I wish donkeys could do this.

Donkeys, donkeys in the deep sea,
Donkeys, donkeys having a cup of tea,
Donkeys, donkeys having a bit of TLC,
How I wish donkeys could do this.

Callum Adair (10)
St Augustine's RC Primary School, Darlington

My Naughty Little Sister

My naughty little sister is called Alice,
She is annoying, grumpy and bossy.
Everyone thinks she's cute
And for her birthday she wants
A dog called Fossy!

She makes mud pies,
She hits and bites,
She is very, very naughty,
And she ripped my favourite tights!

I know she is naughty
But I do love her.
Mum's in hospital,
Now I've got a naughty little brother!

Emily Noble (10)
St Augustine's RC Primary School, Darlington

Monday's Cat

Monday's cat is big and strong
Tuesday's cat can make a good song
Wednesday's cat is small but strong
Thursday's cat can make a pong
Friday's cat is never bad
Saturday's cat is always sad
But the cat that is born on the Sabbath day is sweet,
Cute and loves to eat.

Chloe Outterson (10)
St Augustine's RC Primary School, Darlington

My Favourite Colours!

My favourite colour is pink,
It reminds me of my bear,
My room,
My carpet,
My lucky things and rings.

My favourite colour is purple,
It reminds me of my teddy,
My pen,
My bouncing ball,
My lucky things and rings.

Rosie Pilling (9)
St Augustine's RC Primary School, Darlington

Fantasy World!

My fantasy world would be . . .
Where golden trees grow chocolate leaves
And magical outfits appear out of the air,
Where happiness comes with everything
And no one believes in hatred and war.

The real world is . . .
Where money is hard to earn,
Outfits have to be bought,
Hatred comes with most things
And people have war like they have life.

How we can make a difference . . .
We can save up,
We can wait until we need things,
We can love and care for everyone,
We cannot make war, just love everyone.

Katie Newton (11)
St Augustine's RC Primary School, Darlington

I Like . . .

I like shopping at the mall
To find an outfit for the ball.
I buy a dress, plus it's pink
And it makes the boys wink.

I like make-up to go with my dress,
I put it on good so I don't look a mess.
I love make-up, it's my thing,
I call my friends to give them a ring.

I like clothes
But I hate frills and bows.
Skirts, trousers and tops
That's what I buy from the shops.

I like dogs
But I hate frogs.
Dogs are so cute
I'd buy her some boots.

I like all these things!

Sophie Bainbridge (10)
St Augustine's RC Primary School, Darlington

What's Lurking In The Dark?

What's lurking in the dark . . . a monster with big teeth?
Is it out to get me or to eat me?
What's lurking in the dark . . . a vast spider that will catch me?
What should I do?
What's lurking in the dark . . . a vicious, evil dog with teeth as
                                                    sharp as razors?
I'm stuck in this strange place.
What's lurking in the dark . . . a mysterious face I can't see?
Help me!
What's lurking in the dark . . . a hand that's touching me.
Oh no!
What's lurking in the dark . . . a rhinoceros that's chasing me?
No seriously!
What's lurking in the dark . . . a dreadful noise that's running
                                                    through me.
Argh!
What's lurking in the dark . . . a streak of lightning flashing in
                                                    front of me.
Boom!
I wake up, was it a dream? No it was real, a ghost is staring at me.
'Wake up, wake up,' it's a voice, it was my mam.
Good, it's a dream,
Or was it . . . ?

Laura Hustwick (11)
St Bede's RC Primary School, Darlington

Time!

Twenty-five minutes had now gone,
Still had not got anything done.

Ten minutes later, didn't have anything
In my head at all!

Five minutes later, one thing popped into my mind,
Then more popped into my mind.

Fifteen minutes later, didn't know which one to choose,
Couldn't make my mind up at all.

Twenty minutes, still couldn't make my mind up,
Sir said to 'save your work'.

Two minutes later, didn't know what to do,
I couldn't save any because I didn't do any!

Conner Hamilton (11)
St Bede's RC Primary School, Darlington

Random Thoughts

At the moment I am trying to write a poem,
But I cannot decide on a certain topic to write about.
One minute I've got one idea, the other I've got a totally
                                        different thought.

Now I have nowt!

Suddenly I feel a great idea pop into my head,
Then another and another.
I cannot decide on a subject
As the thoughts in my head are starting to smother.

So now my poem of random thoughts is coming to an end,
But now another great idea is in my head.
Poems are like a cycle,
When you've finished the poem of your choice,
You get another great idea!

Anna Reed (11)
St Bede's RC Primary School, Darlington

Nightmare!

My nightmare is scary, I can't go to sleep,
There's someone outside with big, noisy feet.

Crash, bang, boom, sounds all around in my room.
Screaming and crying in the street.

I can't go to sleep, so I try and count sheep,
But I don't succeed.

I start to cry with a little twinkle in my eye,
I can't go to sleep, there's someone outside.

Loren Bell (11)
St Bede's RC Primary School, Darlington

Chicken

Tommy was a boy no older than ten,
He didn't like his chicken so he gave it to Ben.
Ben was his dog, who was already full,
And he picked it up with a big strong pull.
Ben took it outside and it started to rain
But then a sudden slip and it fell down the drain.
It fell into the sewer and the rats ate away,
And now it has gone for this Saturday.

Adam Tombling (11)
St Bede's RC Primary School, Darlington

The Creature . . .

It was the cry of the creature, the piercing howl of *death!*
It was searching for me - as I hid, I held my breath . . .

I let out all my breath. Oppressed with fear.
Finally it sensed me, grinning from ear to ear.

It leapt at me! Not *ran* - not *crept!*
I couldn't escape sneakily, I ran, not *leapt.*

It grabbed me and slammed me to the floor,
It then began crushing my head . . .

Sadly my life was no more . . .
And before I knew it, I was dead!

So now you've heard my tale of woe,
This is something you'll definitely know,

Never journey into the drain . . .
Or *you'll* never be seen again!

Leon Cunningham (10)
St Bede's RC Primary School, Darlington

Questions

I have so many questions,
So many things to ask, like,
Why is water wet
And why are horses fast?
Why do dogs bark
And why did Noah build an ark?
Why do cats yowl in the night
And why does the dark give me such a fright?
Why is why a question
That so many people ask
And why was writing this poem
Such a difficult task?

Eleanor Thirlway (11)
St Bede's RC Primary School, Darlington

Cutty Sark

On Monday, 21st May, in the very early hours of the day,
The lovely ship, the *Cutty Sark*, was completely destroyed by *arson.*
It went longer than Noah's ark.

The lovely ancient artifacts helped me to learn
What the history of it was about.
Luckily most of the artifacts never got burnt or caught fire
Because a few days earlier, they were taken out.

The solar sails were ripped to pieces; not just the solar sails,
The deck was burnt like the sun was shining on it at 200 degrees.
The nails couldn't hold the deck from the flames.

How could they destroy such a brilliant ship?
'Cause the first time I saw it, it caught my face, even my lip.
It really hurt me when I heard about it.
The good old ship would always hate its new kit.

It hurt the whole of Great Britain, which I'm very sad about.
The fire brigade who got the fire out
Did all they could to help get the fire out.

Goodbye *Cutty Sark,* till spring 2009.

Robert Spereall (11)
St Bede's RC Primary School, Darlington

A Child's Point Of View

(This poem is dedicated to my mum, Tracy Robson)

Mum, you gave me the one thing another mum couldn't,
Life, and most importantly, confidence.
You believed in me when no one else could, not even myself,
You can see the best in people, especially when that person cannot.

Other people, or friends, come and go,
But wherever I am and wherever my mum is,
I know that she is watching and listening
To every breath and step I take.

Teas, breakfasts are what some mums only do,
And you do all those things,
But the best thing you do is love me.

Having a mum like you is like owning a thousand jewels,
You sparkle like the diamonds, you are warm like the topazes,
You are filled with love and care,
So it's like owning all those jewels and a lot, lot more.

Every day I wish that when I grow up I will be just like you,
So when I'm older and anytime my child has fallen over
And she wants me to pick her up,
Or when she's had a bad day at school,
Or every time she wants a hug, I'll think of you.

Real dreams are made up of careful thinking,
A good deal of work and a whole lotta imagination,
My dreams are made of a lotta imagination, yes,
But the best thing my dreams are made of is you.

Sunny days, rainy days, in our house it's never blue,
Even when the day is, because we've got my mum inside our house
And that would make it a sunny day any day of the year.

Day after day you cook, you clean, you hoover,
You look after everything in the house,
And I would hate it if anybody else looked after me.

A day without you is like living a walking, talking nightmare
And now I'd be asking myself who is going to
Tuck me into bed at night and who is going to
Give me a goodnight kiss and who is going to look after me?

You are the one person I want when I've had a bad day at school
And when I have fallen over, I wouldn't want
Anyone else to pick me up but you!

So I'd just like to say, no one could replace you,
Not even another day.

Lucy Robson (10)
St Bede's RC Primary School, Darlington

A Key To My Life

Exit a world of pain and fear,
Get out of my life or I will see ya,
See ya on the other side,
The bad side where corpses rot.

The malicious, vicious and brain-numbing shock
That remained in my mind
Like a murderous lock.

Skulls are buried beneath my feet,
My blood is racing like a flowing beat!

Open the door and get out *quick*
Before your death eddies
With just one hit.

Summer Hanson (10)
St Bede's RC Primary School, Darlington

Or Does It?

It doesn't matter if I drop litter,
Or does it?
It will only cost other people's time to pick it up!

It doesn't matter if I spray patterns on walls,
Or does it?
It will only cost other people's money to clean up!

It doesn't matter if I push or hit,
Or does it?
It will only cost other people's happiness!

It doesn't matter if I kill animals for fun,
Or does it?
It will only cost other creatures their lives!

It doesn't matter if I pollute this Earth,
Or does it?
It will only cost others their future!

It doesn't matter if I do any of these things,
Or does it?
It will only cost me common sense if I didn't!

Rose Passman (11)
St Bede's RC Primary School, Darlington

Greedy Guts!

As the water flows,
I wonder where it goes.
Does it go to sea?
I thought it came to me!

As the birds fly high,
They flap round in the sky.
Do they try to flee?
I thought they came to me!

As the clock ticks the time,
Tickety-tock, tickety-tock is a rhyme.
Does the clock tell all the time?
I thought it was mine!

As a parcel was delivered,
In my boots I shook and quivered.
Open it up and in big letters
Reads, *greedy guts!*

Emma Reid (11)
St Bede's RC Primary School, Darlington

The End Of The World

The rose fell,
The Earth's shell
Breaks into a million pieces.

The glittering moon,
The stars' gloom,
Vanishes into thin air.

The flares of fire burning,
The whole world is turning
Upside down!

Drugs have been destroyed,
We have made the world annoyed,
What have we turned into?

Murderers unite, thinking of plans,
Despite they all turn into ash.

Polar bears, what a shame,
They disappeared down the drain,
But they're back, ready for action.

The court's knocked down,
There is no crown,
The good is back!

Isn't it a shame I can pick out
So many bad things in this world?
But will that change?
We will only see that in time . . .

Kate Blakeborough (11)
St Bede's RC Primary School, Darlington

Mylo

I remember the day I chose you,
You were sat at the back of the cage.
You were the only dog I liked.
All the other dogs were jumpy, but you weren't.
I took you for a walk
All around the rescue centre,
And then it dawned,
You were perfect!
I remember when we went to the photographer's,
You sat by my side,
You just sat there,
Even when the cameras flashed
You just sat there!
I remember at Oakies field
When Daniel dropped the lead,
You ran onto the pitch,
But you came straight back when you were told to.
I remember when you came to sleep at ours,
When you never left my side.
Daniel said it wasn't fair,
When you wouldn't go near him.
I remember you all of the time, Mylo,
You'll never be forgotten, ever!

Andrew Kitchen (11)
St Joseph's RC (VA) Primary School, Stanley

My Grandma

I look at the picture of you and me
And see how happy we are.
I'll treasure for life your wedding ring
And hope to wear it someday.
I miss you, we were like best friends,
Thank you for all your love and care,
I still have you in my heart.
That's how it's meant to be.

Sarah Young (11)
St Joseph's RC (VA) Primary School, Stanley

My Dad

We always used to play,
Every night and every day.
He was there when my life started,
But now we are totally parted.
I still see him once a week,
But me and him hardly speak.
I still love my dad a lot,
Even more now than when I was a tot!

Katy Robson (11)
St Joseph's RC (VA) Primary School, Stanley

My Uncle, Victor

I always used to see you
On a sunny day,
Just chatting to the neighbours.
You always used to love a cup of tea,
But I sure think you loved me.
You always used to put on the lottery,
But didn't always win much.
How you were great to me!

Hannah True (11)
St Joseph's RC (VA) Primary School, Stanley

My Grandma

Sitting there, rocking in that chair,
Remembering memories as she knits,
Thinking of precious times she has been through,
With a pinch of breath she said,
'I am petrified and lonely, but in Heaven I will be free.'
My grandma was face to face with God.

Jack McCrea (11)
St Joseph's RC (VA) Primary School, Stanley

A Dream For Peace

Sitting here I daydream,
Thinking of the world in peace,
No war in Iraq, no war anywhere,
Just love, happiness and friendship!

No war in schools either,
No cliques or enemies!
All together, friends forever,
That's how it should be!

People's lives are saved,
Terrorists are gone,
The army isn't needed,
'Cause no one owns a gun!

Racism, 'What's that?' we say,
That word isn't used in my day!
Unfortunately this is my day,
My world, I made it up!

None of this has happened yet,
But the future's yet to come.
Watch this space, look for my face,
Worldwide Peacemaker!

Emily Wilson-James (11)
St Joseph's RC (VA) Primary School, Stanley

Hilda

Drip, drip, the tears I cry at night,
Thinking about my aunt Hilda, my loss.
I think of her alive, a faded memory.

Heaven is your home now,
God is your neighbour,
This hole in my life shall be filled,
No matter what, no matter where,
You will be there.

Adam Caulfield (10)
St Joseph's RC (VA) Primary School, Stanley

My Dog, Elisear

E is for every day I spent with her
L is for how much she lazed around
I is for I loved her so much
S is for seeing her always
E is for every time she smiled at me
A is for our friendship always
R is for RIP for ever.

Bethany Wilkins (11)
St Joseph's RC (VA) Primary School, Stanley

A Poem For My Gran

I can still remember
All the things you
Have done for me
And all the happy times.

I appreciate all the things
You have given me,
I thank you for everything,
So kind and generous to me.

I will remember you
Being kind to me,
For years to come.

Adam Thompson (11)
St Joseph's RC (VA) Primary School, Stanley

Auntie Elsie

I was only small when you died,
I had only seen you five times,
But in my heart I will still remember you.
You got me the nicest cards and gifts.
Aunty Elsie, I still have
A clear picture of you
In my mind.

Rachael Cowan (11)
St Joseph's RC (VA) Primary School, Stanley

My Grandad

Just to let you know I am OK,
So are my brother, mam and dad.
To Grandad, you make me happy when skies are grey,
You turn the skies bright blue.
Your peaceful life lit the world.

Daniel Connor (11)
St Joseph's RC (VA) Primary School, Stanley

A Poem For My Dog

Scruffy was a dog,
But not only a dog,
She was my dog.

I would walk through the door,
She would be there,
Waiting for me.

I would walk into my room,
She would be there,
Lying waiting for me.

I would walk downstairs,
She would be there,
Lying waiting for me.

I loved my dog, Scruffy,
And she has gone to be with God.
Scruffy, stay there for
We will meet again one day.

Luke Tulip (11)
St Joseph's RC (VA) Primary School, Stanley

Grandad

I hope you're OK Grandad,
I think of you all the time.
I look down in my heart
And I know you're still alive.
I think of you morning to night,
See you in the beautiful stars.
I'll never let you go.

Andrew Connor (11)
St Joseph's RC (VA) Primary School, Stanley

A Memorial Poem To John Barker

John was a great man with a great personality.
He was a great grandad,
Had a sense of humour,
Not noisy or boisterous.
He was also kind, gentle.
His death shocked us,
Our family was sad and depressed,
We could hardly cope.
We tried to help, he was consumed in death.
Suddenly he had passed out of our hands,
But his spirit and memories still live on in us!

Jonathan Grey (11)
St Joseph's RC (VA) Primary School, Stanley

The Brave Rabbit

Once in a forest lived a proud-headed lion,
He annoyed and killed a lot of animals daily
And thus he had a great time for days, weeks and months.

The animals were exhausted by the lion,
They wanted an end to this
So they gathered up.

The decision they took was,
Daily, one animal would go to the den.
The lion also compromised with it.

The fateful day came for the rabbit,
As everyone, he was also scared to face death.
On his way to the den he prayed to God.

He was too thirsty, then saw a well nearby.
He looked into the well and suddenly he thought of an idea!
He ran to the den rather late.

The lion was really angry.
He roared and asked, 'Why are you late?'
With great respect the rabbit said, 'It's a great story,'
And explained humbly,

'On my way I saw a lion just like you
And he said that he was king of the forest.
He chased me and I hardly escaped.'

The lion shook his mane and stood with all his power.
He roared and asked, 'Where is he?'
The rabbit said politely, 'Come with me and I will show you.'

The rabbit pointed to the well and said, 'He lives there.'
The lion looked at the well and saw the other one.
He roared and jumped into it.

The foolish lion didn't realise it was his reflection
He saw in the well!
Thus the small brain brought peace to the big forest.

Shalu James (10)
St William's RC (VA) Primary School, Trimdon Station

Pets

Dogs, cats, birds and more,
White mice sitting at the house door.
Under water, in the air,
You need to take a lot of care.

Taking the dog for a walk in the wood,
It bounces in a lot of mud.
Birds are sitting in a tree,
Flying by is a bumblebee.

Rabbits hop in their hutch,
In the garden, they eat too much.
Dogs, cats, birds and more,
So many animals, I will never bore.

Elise Brown (9)
St William's RC (VA) Primary School, Trimdon Station

Fairies, Fairies Everywhere!

Fairies, fairies everywhere
On a branch or in the air!
Flying free and flying high
In the summer's clear blue sky.

Fairies, fairies everywhere,
On a branch or in the air!
The fairy that has golden wings
Wears silver and diamond sparkly rings.

Fairies, fairies everywhere,
On a branch or in the air!

Alix Payne (9)
St William's RC (VA) Primary School, Trimdon Station

My Life, My Magic Box

(Inspired by 'Magic Box' by Kit Wright)

A place where I can swim the seven seas,
A place where I can buzz with the bees,
A place where I can run and glide,
A place where I can seek and hide,
A place where I can never get chickenpox,
My magic box . . . my magic box.

Emeka Ononeze (10)
St William's RC (VA) Primary School, Trimdon Station

Please Mr Lion

(Inspired by 'Please Mrs Butler' by Alan Ahlberg)

Please Mr Lion,
This dog, Tippy Tall,
Keeps pulling my fur, Sir
And I don't like it at all.

Go jump in the river,
Go swim in the sea,
Go do something quickly
Before it is tea.

Please Mr Lion,
This bunny, Hippety-Hop,
Keeps spilling my pop
And I hate it a lot.

Go buy some pop
And share it with Hippety-Hop,
Go buy a hammer
And hit her with a mop.

Basma Cherradi (9)
St William's RC (VA) Primary School, Trimdon Station

Dare Not Take A Breath

There was a cold breeze
Blowing through her hair,
She was not breathing,
She did not dare.

I wonder why
She would be
Stood so still
Gazing out to sea.

Her pale skin
And eyes so deep
Made you wonder
Did she sleep?

She stood there
Like she was lost at sea,
A queen in white,
She stood there peacefully.

The queen that stood still
Dare not take a breath,
She is the queen
And the wife of death . . .

Rebecca Dentith (10)
St William's RC (VA) Primary School, Trimdon Station

What Am I?

Their eyes sparkle
In the dead of night.
They are your fluffy alarm clock,
Which wakes you when the cockerel crows.
They will be your friend forever,
Someone who will always be there for you.

What am I?
A: A cat.

Jessica Storey (11)
St William's RC (VA) Primary School, Trimdon Station

Friend

I saw my friend on a big slide,
Should I jump? I couldn't decide.
No need! She came up to meet me,
I hate it when people stand so you can't see.
It always happens in the fair,
I told my mum I didn't care.
It is better than sitting at home,
No one is in, so I am all alone.

How about we go to my house?
I need to clean up the dead mouse
That my cat killed last night,
I tell you, it wasn't a nice sight.
If my mum is in a good mood she'll do it,
I would put on an old shirt or football kit.

Unless we can find an excuse not to!
I know, I will visit my Auntie Sue.
It might not be fun,
But it's better than roasting in the sun.
I might, just might, clean up the mouse,
Then my mum will let us in the house!

Brad Langley Thompson (10)
St William's RC (VA) Primary School, Trimdon Station

The Dream

I went to bed
One summer's night,
Everything was dark
Except for one light.

The light of the moon
Glistening on my bed,
I watched it for hours
Until I laid down my weary head.

Suddenly I was in a world,
A world of wonderful things,
From games and toys for girls and boys
And even cars that sing!

Then creatures came from other towns,
Cities and even space,
Their names were Freddie, Jason, Debbie
And the mighty Leather Face.

They saw my face,
I trembled with fear,
Then I said to myself,
'I wish I was not here.'

They ran towards me,
Hurling stones,
One hit my chest,
I tried to stop my groans.

Then I woke up,
It was a dream,
Then I noticed a mark on my chest
And then I started to *scream!*

Martin Worthington (11)
St William's RC (VA) Primary School, Trimdon Station

If I Were A Footballer

If I were a footballer, I'd score and win the league.
If I were a footballer, I'd captain the England team.
If I were a footballer, I'd break the back of the net.
If I were a footballer, I'd never be in debt.
If I were a footballer, I'd never foul or cheat.
If I were a footballer, I'd never get beat.
If I were a footballer, I'd take penalties and free kicks.
If I were a footballer, I'd never eat a chocolate Twix.
But I am not a footballer and I'm sat here with the flu,
But I know I can do what I do.

Matthew Bennett (11)
St William's RC (VA) Primary School, Trimdon Station

Bullying

I've seen what it's like to be bullied,
Thumped and pushed about.
I've seen what it's like to be bullied,
Bullies won't stop when you shout.

I know what it's like to be bullied,
Scared to go outside.
I know what it's like to be bullied,
Confused, lonely, you hide.

I've heard what it's like to be bullied,
Being kicked and scarred for life.
I've heard what it's like to be bullied,
Sometimes threatened with a knife.

I can feel what it's like to be bullied,
Stared at in the street.
I can feel what it's like to be bullied,
Muttered about by everyone you meet.

I've been told what it's like to be bullied,
Pounded and punched as you cry.
I've been told what it's like to be bullied,
Hiding behind your hands because you're shy.

I know what it's like to be bullied,
After all, it has happened to me.
I know what it's like to be bullied,
But I told someone and now I'm happy.

Ciaran Jasper (11)
St William's RC (VA) Primary School, Trimdon Station

A Car Journey

My car is a Ford,
My sister is getting bored,
Playing with her old games.

When it is night,
It is like driving
Through a field of headlights.

My brother has a car,
Also, he gave me a chocolate bar,
Munch!

Mum is driving,
Now my sister is crying,
She is saying, 'Are we there yet?'

I am starving,
'Can we go to McDonald's?'
But are we there yet?

Mark Ellis (11)
St William's RC (VA) Primary School, Trimdon Station

Why?

Why is a word that means
A lot of things,
Such as questions.

Why is a begging word,
Or just to get your own way.
Your mam and dad say, 'What are you doing?'
And you just say, 'Why?'

You use it in your daily life,
You use this word every day,
So let's say it again,
Why? Why? Why?

I wish you were here with me
When I say the word.
I don't care what you say,
All I will say is, 'Why? Why? Why?'

I love saying it every day
And every night,
It's a lot of fun.
All you have to do is say the special word,
'Why?'

Harry Sheldon (10)
St William's RC (VA) Primary School, Trimdon Station

Young Writers - Little Laureates Poems From Co Durham

Water

Water
Is so
Nice.
How
It splashes
Down
The
Waterfall.
It is so
Interesting
How
The water
Evaporates
Into the
Atmosphere.
Water vapour
Makes
Clouds.
The clouds
Burst to
Make *rain!*

John Ashurst (11)
St William's RC (VA) Primary School, Trimdon Station

Dr Fruit

Hi, I'm Dr Fruit, but I'm a strawberry
That's quite extraordinary
One nibble of me and you'll be disease-free
I don't know why I'm also in the FBI
Oh why must I be in the FBI?

Yes, I'm a secret spy
I have a car that can fly
I always stop the thief
But I also stop for a brief.

My boss will kill me
If he knew I told ye
So do you hear?
Because murderer's here.

Mark Allaway (9)
St William's RC (VA) Primary School, Trimdon Station

Budgies

Budgies go cheep, cheep, cheep,
They love shiny stuff,
Budgies are very colourful,
They have sharp claws.

And every day they go cheep,
We take the budgies everywhere,
They eat lots a day,
Ah, they're gone!

They've gone to Australia
And now to Mexico.
The budges are back
For their tea.

Liam Cairns-Smith (9)
St William's RC (VA) Primary School, Trimdon Station

As Wide As Space

As wide as space, an open window
To another dimension but nobody knows
What that wide holds and you are aboard.

As wide as an open window,
Black dimension wider than your imagination.
I want to explore Mars, a red, dusty, deserted planet and
a frosty orb,
But I think that window will never be opened.

I only gaze out of that now,
I think one day I might explore more and more.
One day it will be.

Joseph Worley (10)
St William's RC (VA) Primary School, Trimdon Station

Doctor, Doctor

Doctor, Doctor, I am very sick!
Please tick me off as your sick list.
Please, if you don't, I'll die at home,
So tick me off your sick list, please.
Help, help, help Doctor,
I think I am dying right now,
So tick me off your list.

Courtney Turnbull (9)
St William's RC (VA) Primary School, Trimdon Station

The Football Match!

Gazing at the TV,
Waiting for the first kick,
Mummy's here, Daddy's there,
Oh, you have missed it.

Jumping on my knees,
Clashing my head,
Oh my goodness, there's a touch
Of class, *kerching!*

I am now on the pitch,
Ready to kick some?
This time I have
Won it for us.

That's not all,
That's not all, this time
I have scored a wonder goal.

But that's not all . . .
Granny Grunt's legs have fallen off.
Five . . . four . . . three . . . two . . . one . . .
Blast off! Goal!

Jordan Gavin (11)
St William's RC (VA) Primary School, Trimdon Station

My Grandma

My grandma is great,
My grandma is kind,
Embarrassing sometimes,
But I don't mind!

We make cakes,
She drinks tea
And Grandma makes
Hot chocolate for me!

We go on trips
And have ice cream.
Grandma takes me on walks
And it feels like a dream!

We play games,
Grandma gives me sweets,
Biscuits, cakes
And lots of tasty treats!

So whenever you need
A hug or a kiss,
Just go to your grandma
And you will have your day's wish!

Sarah Cant (11)
St William's RC (VA) Primary School, Trimdon Station

My Little Dolls' House

I have a little dolls' house
I play with every day,
But when I ask for dolly,
She says, 'Go away!'

The mother of my dolls' house
Is washing in the sink,
So when I ask a question
She says, 'I'll have to think.'

I ask if they want a picnic
Or go on a trip today,
But all they ever say to me is,
'I don't want to play.'

Unfortunately it looks to me
My toys don't seem to hear,
But even so I love them
And will always keep them near.

Rebecca Spellman (10)
St William's RC (VA) Primary School, Trimdon Station

Young Writers Information

We hope you have enjoyed reading this book - and that you will continue to enjoy it in the coming years.

If you like reading and writing poetry drop us a line, or give us a call, and we'll send you a free information pack.

Alternatively if you would like to order further copies of this book or any of our other titles, then please give us a call or log onto our website at www.youngwriters.co.uk

Young Writers Information
Remus House
Coltsfoot Drive
Peterborough
PE2 9JX

(01733) 890066